T0114872

THE MISSING ELEMENT

LEVORN DANIELS

authorHOUSE®

AuthorHouse™
1663 Liberty Drive
Bloomington, IN 47403
www.authorhouse.com
Phone: 833-262-8899

© 2020 Levorn Daniels. All rights reserved.

No part of this book may be reproduced, stored in a retrieval system, or transmitted by any means without the written permission of the author.

Published by AuthorHouse 09/18/2020

ISBN: 978-1-6655-0007-4 (sc)
ISBN: 978-1-6655-0097-5 (e)

Print information available on the last page.

Any people depicted in stock imagery provided by Getty Images are models, and such images are being used for illustrative purposes only. Certain stock imagery © Getty Images.

This book is printed on acid-free paper.

Because of the dynamic nature of the Internet, any web addresses or links contained in this book may have changed since publication and may no longer be valid. The views expressed in this work are solely those of the author and do not necessarily reflect the views of the publisher, and the publisher hereby disclaims any responsibility for them.

Everyday millions of customers will make the drastic choice to take their business to a competitor of the business they currently use. These customers are the lifeline of the companies that they utilize. The glue that keeps them stuck to your company is the customer service agent that serves on the front line who interacts with every one of the customers whether it is face-to-face, via telephone or internet. These interactions are extremely crucial to the business in terms of maintaining the customer base and moreover in terms of expanding the customer base. These interactions even determine the longevity of the business.

We will explore basic techniques on how to handle customer interactions from the beginning unto the ending. The general process can be applied face-to-face, via telephone or internet. The goal is not to shape the representative into a cloned robot. It is simply a guide to give direction to the agent. There are countless ways to assist a customer. Most of the techniques can be effective. One can travel to Washington, DC from St. Louis by traveling westward, but you would have to travel around the world to get there. This guide is to prepare the agent to achieve greater efficiency.

I have done door-to-door insurance sales, retail mobile phone sales and store management, auto sales along with cable television bundle services. Enjoying success in each step along the way, I learned patterns through the school of hard knocks that carry over regardless of the corporation or product/service that can be applied with great results. I am sharing my wealth of knowledge and experience I learned from trial and error and developed while employed in the workplace with Fortune 500 corporations including Sprint and Comcast. The result will prevent unnecessary customer and agent frustration and customer migration to the competition.

CHOOSE CAREER CAREFULLY

Customer service agents have an extremely important responsibility in assisting and retaining customers. A good agent can retain a customer base. The opposite holds true for a bad representative. In choosing a job, it is extremely imperative to make sure before taking a position in customer care that you have the right make up mentally to adequately fill the job. You first decide if you are right for customer service and if customer service is right for you. If you do land in the field and realize it is not for you check the availability of switching to another position within the organization. Speak to management to find a position more geared for your qualities and abilities. Lateral moves often are perfect for the company and employee. The company can retain you as a representative filling an opening without recruiting anyone else. Your time is much too valuable to waste doing a job that will be tedious to you if you do not enjoy assisting the public. Also, the customers are far too valuable to the business to encounter anyone who is not interested in assisting them. One lack luster or bad experience can be very costly and damage the brand of the business.

PREPARE PHYSICALLY AND MENTALLY

So, you have selected a new career, or you are striving to become better at what you do professionally. The first step is just common sense. Make sure you are well groom for your job. Be on top of your hygiene. A smart thing to do if you work face to face with customers is to keep breath mints in case something you eat turns on you or if you have any type of illness that can cause odor. Know your body so that you can overcome challenges. For example: I worked wearing suits in the South even in the summer. I used a combination of body spray with baby powder to prevent or reduce sweating. Dress the part for your job. Perception is major. It is almost impossible to overcome a negative first impression. Consequently, make sure your uniform looks professional whether it is a suit or a polo shirt and khakis. Do not wear stained or wrinkled clothes.

Next, make sure you are rested and nourished. You do not want to be sleepy or fatigue. If you are not fully alert or rested, your customers can pick up on it, and it can negatively impact your experience with your customers. Sleepiness will reduce your better judgement, listening skills and response time. Again, know your body and the amount of sleep your body requires to operate efficiently. Your customers deserve to have you at your best physically and mentally.

GREET AND MEET

The most important element in each transaction will take place within the initial moments. Most experts will agree that the tone must be set in the greet and meet. Face-to-face, this aspect of the interaction engulfs the personal appearance of the agent including body language and hygiene. One can speak volumes without uttering a word. The customer can pick-up on a negative vibe that cannot be overcome regardless of what is said by negative body language. Be sure that all body language is positive with the appearance of being interested in engaging with the customer regardless of your view of the customer. Be natural and let your persona flow outward. Listen for clues of the customer's personality and adapt to it. For example: if the customer is straight forward be sure to stick to the business at hand. Remember people like to do business with likeminded individuals. Mirror your customer.

EMPATHY

Now that you have had a successful needs assessment, place yourself in your customer's shoes and think like your customer. Feel the customer's frustration and anxiety. Be empathic unto the customer. The customer is not always right. However, the customer indirectly owns your business and without the customer there is no need for the business. Think of the customer as the individual paying your salary. You will not be able to please each customer, but you can be empathic to each customer. Feedback from customers is extremely important. Only a very small percentage of customers will voice opinions or complaints regardless of medium whether thru surveys or direct approach. Most disappointed customers will tell a minimum twenty people about their negative experience or what they view as being negative. With today's social media, a negative view can snowball via email chain letter, tweet or post on a social site where thousands of people can know of the occurrence within minutes. Therefore, it is extremely imperative to nip any negative views immediately with the utmost integrity to avoid potentially harmful misrepresentation of the company. The best way to do this to make sure the customer knows upfront you empathize for him or her and will gladly assist him or her. Remember that being empathetic is not stating a canned script. Empathy is making the customer's need the priority. Be genuine. Flow naturally.

NEEDS ASSESSMENT

One of the most important elements in properly assisting a customer is the needs assessment. The needs assessment is the process of finding out what needs to be addressed with the customer. This is where the agent and customer fuse on the same page in terms of resolving the issue faced by the customer. The way to this is through proper fact-finding. In this step you will ask who, what, when, where and how. Do not make assumptions as to what the customer is thinking or confronting. Ask the customer open ended questions to get feedback. Confirm what the customer is seeking back to the customer within the initial moments to prevent wasting your and the customers time. It is best to take an extra minute or two upfront before any actions are taken and get the correct understanding of what is needed than finding out later after wasting time and resources. Wasted time and money frustrates customers and can be overwhelming financially and resource wise to the business. Before any actions are taken be sure you and the customer agree regarding solutions presented to them.

LISTEN

Ensure you give your best to assisting your customer. Remove all distractions including managers and co-workers. In today's corporate environment often, representatives are trying to assist customers while receiving company memos, email, instant messages and etcetera. It is easy to lose focus on the customer you are assisting by thinking of timelines to be met, meetings to attend, other employees and management monitoring your conversation and the other customers waiting to be assisted. These distractions pose an injustice to the customer you are assisting. To adequately listen to the customer, all distractions need to be eliminated. Give your undivided attention to the customer you are assisting. You can only efficiently assist one customer at a time. Listen to the tone of voice and observe physical messages if you can see the customer. Non-verbal messages speak volume. Practice active listening by repeating back to the customer what you think you heard to be sure you are on the same page. It is best to do this early in the transaction than to fine out later you were not in sync on the same page. Do not make assumptions of what you believe the customer is saying. The customer may state one thing with the best of intention to explain it to you correctly, but it may come out the direct opposite of what is said. Be sure you have a clear understanding on the objective of the customer. Keep in mind that the customer should be doing most of the talking in this step. Acknowledge feedback whether it is a complaint or compliment.

Avoid interrupting customers as much possible. Not allowing the customer to speak his or her frustration adds fuel to the fire. Allowing the customer to vent diffuses a volatile or negative situation. Listen for clues to discover needs and problems. Steer the customer towards obtaining positive feedback and information needed to get to the solution. Avoid endless ranting that leads to nothing constructive and the wasting of your and the customer's time by guiding the conversation.

TAKE OWNERSHIP

Take ownership of any issue that rise. Position yourself as a friend and not simply a representative. Insurance agents are required to have errors and omissions insurance because they are an extension of the company. Be like insurance agents and know that you are the expert. You are the company. Resolve the customer's concern as quick as possible. If you must get assistance from another representative or another department stay with the customer and inform the next agent of what has transpired with good details pertaining to the customer's needs. If you are in a call center setting and must get help from another individual or department do a warm transfer of the customer to the next representative. Give the customer assurance that he or she is in good hands and will not have to deal with the process of explaining anything to anyone else. If possible, follow up with the customer in an appropriate time to make sure the customer was taken care of.

PRESENT SOLUTION

Ask the customer for assistance with developing a plan of action or proposal. Involve the customer in the solution. Do not focus on or mention what you cannot do. Focus on what you can do and offer a suggestion with solving the customer's needs as the primary objective. Too often, agents present options with their own interest in the form of commission or accomplishment at the forefront. Be the problem solver who develops a long-term approach. Place the customer interest ahead of personal goals or ambition. Present a solution based upon the customer's input with confidence. Do not appear as if you are not knowledgeable of what you are doing or convinced in your own capacity to take care of the customer with the solution. Companies are in business to make profit and people work for salary. However, there is a happy medium. Customers are not opposed to businesses making a profit or you the agent receiving a commission. Many customers will ask the representatives if they will be rewarded for their assistance to assure adequate compensation. The flip side of the coin is that no one wants to pay more than what he or she feels is a fair amount for a product or service. Think of the future potential business of repeat sales and referrals. Keep in mind that some customers will not be pleased with any solution. Others try to get over on companies. The goal is to find a happy medium that is mutually good for both the customer and the company. Importantly, do not think sales incentive, commission or spiff first when it comes to selling. Put yourself in the customer's seat. Compensation will come in time.

KEEP SIMPLE

Always use the KISS technique (keep it simple stupid). Avoid over complicating. Geometry teaches that a straight line between two points is the shortest distance between them. Likewise, in customer service, you should always be straight forward. It is the best process. Do not over complicate. Approach the customers' concern directly with the simplest approach towards resolving the apparent issue. As taught in speech, analyze the individual you are assisting and speak to the individual on the individuals' level. Never try to impress the person being assisted by speaking in company jargon. If the customer does not know what you are saying in business terms, it is frugal and pointless.

DISCLOSE DETAILS

Disclose all details and give full disclosure prior to starting any transaction. Confirm what has been done upon completion. Be up front with customer. Do not conceal information. Reiterate what has been done and what the customer can expect regarding his/her service or product. Giving the full details may spark more initial questioning and concern from the customer, which can eliminate future problems. It is best to make sure the customer has a good understanding of his/her service or products. Full disclosure can prevent churn and charge backs.

Most importantly, full disclosure will educate the customer and help prevent the customer from having future problems, disappointment, concern and questions.

BE QUICK AND EFFICIENT

Customers will spend vast amounts of time from weeks to months researching and comparing companies, products and services. However, when the customers decide to finally buy regardless of how long it took them to contemplate their decisions, you have a short window of time to complete the sales transaction. A large percentage of customers will get very anxious during the time that you are finalizing the sale. Make sure you keep the customers updated on what you are doing during every step of the process to prevent the customers from getting frustrated and backing out. Have a since of urgency and make the closing a quick and simple process. Remember the cliché that time is an ultimate sale killer. Don't let time kill yours!

HAVE FUN

Do not make assisting people into work. Do not be robotic. Keep it a service. Relax. Have fun!!! Build rapport with your customers. Discuss a common interest like a hobby or sports team. Refrain from anything that can be controversial like politics and religion. People enjoy doing business with people who are not up tight or nervous. If you develop a common interest, it will help ease your and the customers' anxiety. Be patient. Enjoy your customers and the experience of the moment with everyone.

THANK

No one likes to be taken for granted. Customers are taken for granted every day. Customers have more and more options for spending their hard-earned money. The difference between many products and services are virtually unnoticeable. Those products and services can be purchased through many channels. The marketplace is extremely competitive and gets even more competitive every day. The only thing that separates the differences effectively now is the customer service. Customers that choose to transact with your business should always be treated with the best service. Moreover, you always thank the customer for patronizing you. Never take the customer's business for granted. I frequently eat in Chinese restaurants. Often the servers can speak very little English. However, they all will tell you, 'Thank you.' Thanking your customer should always be the norm. They indirectly own your business and sign your paycheck by purchasing your product or service. Kroger places a slogan on its paystubs, "This check was made possible by a happy customer." Kroger nailed it! Indeed, customers make employee salaries possible. Do not cut the salaries by cutting the customers.

FOLLOW UP

This step is crucial in getting the customer to enjoy the experience with you, which can lead to repeat sells, good surveys and referrals. Give an expectation of what the customer can expect including a timetable of everything that is to take place. If anything goes unexpected give the customer a courtesy call to inform the customer of what is going on and how unexpected delays or issues will be resolved. With major purchases, it is alright to follow up multiple times after the initial sale if it is not at a frequency that annoys the customer. Be mindful of the customer's schedule. If the customer asks not to be disturbed respect the customer's request.

MASTER YOUR CRAFT

Be a student of your profession. Add as many tools to your tool belt as possible by always learning new techniques. Learn as much about your product or service as possible. Know why what you offer is better than your rival or the alternative of not buying. Observe the best representatives in your field as they perform. Be mindful that sometimes the best is at a rival. If you can observe them do so. Mystery shop them. Do not mimic them, but look for styles, approaches, and ways of assisting customers that you can adapt into a style that you are comfortable with in your presentation. Read manuals and books on customer traits, tendencies and personalities. Learn to recognize different personalities and how to mesh with them to optimize their experience. Learn from each of your interactions and transactions with your customers. Each interaction and transaction are its own separate entity. There are no two alike. You should analyze what you did right and wrong and how in a similar situation you can give the next customer a better experience. However, do not dwell on any transaction whether it was a good or subpar experience. Take an athlete's approach to your skill set and mentality. Know your strengths and weakness. Maximize your strengths and minimize your weakness. Regardless of the behavior of the customer remain professional. Never stereotype or shortchange your customers. Keep personal beliefs to yourself. Leave personal issues at home. Give each customer your best effort. Your customers deserve your best. Be the Michael

Jordan of your occupation…the best. Moreover, you should take on the mentality that I am not just the best at what I do but I am my own manager. Gain the knowledge and make the connections that you need to resolve any problem that may come up on your own. Take care any issue without deferring to someone else whenever possible. Remember that most supervisors were promoted to that position because of their mindset, work ethics and knowledge.

ASSISTING IRATE CUSTOMERS

One of the most challenging fears of assisting customers deal with irate customers. Customers can be challenging. They may pout, degrade the business and customer representatives, yell and use profanities. Retail agents occasionally endure physical threats from customers. Sometimes customers take to these antics to bluff representatives into giving in to their demands. The best method of assisting them is not to fight fire with fire. The best technique is to remain kind. Use a modest voice tone and pitch to speak to the upset customer. Typically, the customers will calm down if you remain in control of the situation and calm. Assure the customers you will do what is within your means to assist the customers and continue your normal process. Do not make exceptions for a rude customer and give in to demands of the customer. Doing more than you suppose to do or have already informed the customer you can do will only revoke your credibility. Moreover, it will send a message to the customer that being rude will get him or her any demand he or she has. Also, the news could spread to other customers to do the same antics to get whatever they want. Remember you will not be able to satisfy everyone. Stay professional. Do your best. That is all anyone can do. Do not lose your control. This will cause the negativity to heighten and the situation could spin out of control. If you do lose control of the situation seek assistance from a co-worker or supervisor.

CAUTIOUSLY SELECT CUSTOMERS

Often agents are eager to sell a customer. Although customers are needed to fund business, the wrong customer for the incorrect product or service can be detrimental to the business. While employed with Sprint, I observed the district manager assist a customer who entered the establishment. The customer lived in an extremely rural area where she wanted to use the service. The district manager directly told the customer she needed to get service with a company that serviced her area and named the best company to fulfill her needs. The lesson is to do a need assessment and honestly steer the customer to what is best for the customer even if it is the competition. Many problems businesses and representatives have come from acquiring customers that the business is not suited to efficiently service. Do not offer any option to customers that will lead to problems knowingly. Remember the customer is looking to you the professional in your field to offer and do what is best for him or her. Even if the customer does not buy from you today, the customer may purchase from you in the future or send you referrals. Have integrity.

RELEASING A CUSTOMER

No one likes break ups. Breaking up is hard in a relationship between individuals in a personal relationship. It is the same way with business relationships between representatives and customers. Typically, no one wants to break up with someone that you care about. Unfortunately, some cases warrant the breakup when there is no natural fit or satisfactory benefit to the relationship. You need to set some customers free for their and your company's good to allow another vendor better suited to assisting the customer to acquire the customer. Releasing a customer is the last resort. When it is apparent that it cannot be avoided, be sure to handle the matter with the utmost dignity. Handle the situation in a professional manner with class. Remember the customer may not be the right mesh for a provider-client relationship today but depending on the circumstance may be the best customer for your business in the future. The client could be a source of referrals for your business even while being a customer of a rival business. You will be appreciated and respected for your honesty. You cannot retain all customers. Customers who are not profitable to the company and customers who only speak negative things about the company in a derogatory manner need to find a company where they will be happy. Help those who want to be helped or saved.

AVOID BURNOUT/REDUCE STRESS

Often employees work overtime to increase income by working additional hours. However, this is not always the best way to increase income. Jobs that involve high stress levels should not be extended on a regular basis to extra hours. It is more productive to simply work the required work schedule. If your job offers incentives such as bonuses and commission, focus on quality of your work performance to increase your income through the incentives in place in lieu of countless hours working. You are a better agent when thoroughly rested physically and mentally, which will lead to increased productivity. Have a vital life away from your job and avoid taking your work home. Stay fresh so your performance will be better.

ASSISTING ANOTHER AGENT'S CUSTOMER

Retail and sales consultants often encounter customers that their colleagues have been assisting. If and when a customer is met that needs assistance for a customer service related issue if you can help the customer and have the means and time to do so..do so. Take care of the customer as a courtesy and it will come back to you as good deed. Do not blow the customer off. Put yourself in the customer's shoes and remember that you are a customer for someone as well. Remember that it takes team work to make the dream work. On the flip side of the coin, do not steal a customer where sales commissions and quotas are involved. Sales can be and is cut-throat in environments where incentives including money and awards are involved. Keep the Golden Rule in mind. Do unto others as you would want done unto you. No one would want someone to steal their customer that could be the difference between being able to pay your bills or falling short with paying ones bills or even winning a company award.

WRAP UP

Studies have showed that only a small percentage of customers will notify a business of their displeasure with the business before switching to an alternative business for their needs. Consequently, you must take care of the customers who verbalize to you and listen to them for what they have to say to make sure they are taken care of and pleased to the best of your ability. Make a positive image with each opportunity. Do your due diligence to take care of each customer regardless of the scenario. Take care of your customers and your customers will take care of you.

Happy selling!!! Enjoy your job!!!

The contents of this book are the sole ownership of and copyright protected by Levorn Daniels. All rights are reserved.

Printed in the United States
By Bookmasters